EMERGENCY
INFORMATION

Name . . . .

Address . . . .

Telephone . . . .

Blood Group . . . .

Medical Conditions . . . .

Allergies . . . .

EMERGENCY

FIRST AID

SIENA

First published 1996 by Parragon Book Service Limited, Unit 13-17, Avonbridge Trading Estate, Atlantic Road, Avonmouth, Bristol, BS11 9QD in arrangement with Bloomsbury Publishing Plc.

A Siena Book
Siena is an imprint of Parragon Books

Copyright ©1996 Parragon Books
A copy of the CIP entry for this book is available from the British Library.

ISBN 0 75251 733 3
10 9 8 7 6 5 4 3 2 1

Edited by Isabelle Auden
Designed by Simon Levy Associates
Printed in Italy

HOW TO USE THIS BOOK

The aim of this book is to provide the basic essentials of first aid in an uncomplicated, accessible manner. In the first section is an A-Z of the most common emergency situations and conditions. It covers the ways in which you can recognize them and indicates, step-by-step, what you need to do about it.

 indicates a condition which is potentially life-threatening

italic indicates a cross-reference to another condition or procedure which is covered elsewhere in the book

The end section covers the essential emergency procedures, such as the recovery position, artificial ventilation and cardiopulmonary resuscitation. But don't wait for an emergency to happen – make sure you read this section (preferably the entire book) and familiarize yourself with first-aid techniques now.

Part 1

A – Z
OF DISORDERS
AND INJURIES

ANAPHYLACTIC SHOCK ⚠

What to look out for:
- **difficulty in breathing**
- **rapid pulse**
- **red, blotchy skin rash**
- **swelling of face and neck**
- **puffy eyes**

What to do:

1 Send for an ambulance.

2 Sit the casualty down and help them find a position which enables them to breathe comfortably.

3 If they become unconscious, put them in the *recovery position*, monitor their breathing and pulse, and be ready to start *artificial ventilation* or *cardiopulmonary resuscitation*, if necessary.

BITES AND STINGS

ANIMAL BITES

What to look out for:
- bleeding
- puncture wound, possibly quite deep

What to do:

1 Wash the wound thoroughly under cool running water.

2 Pat dry and cover with a sterile dressing.

3 If the bite is deep, control bleeding by applying direct pressure and raising the affected limb.

4 Ensure that the casualty is taken to hospital.

INSECT STINGS

What to look out for:

- swelling
- pain
- *anaphylactic shock* (in rare cases)

What to do:

1 If the sting is still embedded, remove it with tweezers.

2 Apply a cold compress to ease the swelling.

3 If the pain and swelling continues over the next day or so, advise the casualty to seek medical help.

IMPORTANT: if there is an extreme allergic reaction treat the casualty for *anaphylactic shock.*

EXTERNAL BLEEDING

What to look out for:
- bleeding wound
- *shock*

What to do:

1 Apply direct pressure with your hand, making sure there are no embedded objects in the wound.

2 Apply a sterile dressing or clean pad to the wound.

3 If possible, raise and support the injured limb.

4 Leaving the original dressing in place, bandage it securely.

5 Treat the casualty for *shock*.

IMPORTANT: If there is an object embedded in the wound, do not apply direct pressure but press firmly on either side of the object. When bandaging, build up either side of the object with sterile pads high enough to clear it, so you can secure the bandage without pressing down on the object.

IMPORTANT: Don't waste time on finding pressure points and don't use a tourniquet, as this can lead to gangrene.

INTERNAL BLEEDING

What to look out for:
- cold, pale, clammy skin
- weak and rapid pulse
- pain
- thirst
- confusion
- unconsciousness
- coughing up blood
- blood in the urine or faeces
- severe bruising

What to do:

1 Treat the casualty for *shock* by lying them down and raising their legs.

2 Send for an ambulance and monitor the casualty's breathing and pulse. Be ready to start *artificial ventilation* or *cardiopulmonary resuscitation*, if necessary.

IMPORTANT: be careful not to over-heat casualty. If they complain of being cold, only use one blanket.

ASTHMA

What to look out for:
- difficulty in breathing
- rapid, shallow and noisy breaths
- coughing and wheezing
- tightness in the chest
- distress
- difficulty in speaking
- blue lips and/or skin (in severe cases)

What to do:

1 Sit the casualty down, making sure they lean forward slightly, preferably resting on a support such as a table.

2 Most asthma sufferers carry a 'puffer'. Help them to use it (about 4 puffs).

3 If the casualty's condition does not improve after 10 minutes, give them a further 4 puffs.

ASTHMA

4 If there is still no improvement or if the casualty has no medication and the attack is prolonged, call an ambulance.

IMPORTANT: if this is a first attack, the casualty should see their doctor.

Remember the priorities:

ABC

Airways

Breathing
and
Circulation

CHOKING ⓘ

What to look out for:
- **difficulty in breathing and breathing**
- **blue lips and skin**
- **coughing**
- **inability to speak or cough (in extreme cases)**
- **unconsciousness**

What to do:

1 Let the casualty cough. If difficulty in breathing continues, send for an ambulance.

2 Get behind casualty and put your arms around them, just above the waist, making a fist with one hand and grasping it with the other.

3 Pull sharply inwards and upwards. Repeat as necessary.

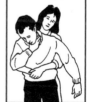

BREATHING DIFFICULTIES

4 If the casualty becomes unconscious lie them on their back, sit astride them and place one hand on top of the other, just below their ribcage. Thrust upwards and inwards.

5 If the casualty's breathing returns, put them in the *recovery position* and monitor their breathing and pulse until help arrives.

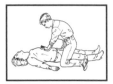

IMPORTANT: if breathing stops, begin artificial ventilation immediately.

IMPORTANT: if the casualty is able to move or cough, don't slap casualty their back, as this may cause the obstruction to shift and block the airway completely.

BABIES AND SMALL CHILDREN: place these across your lap, face down and head low, giving them 5 sharp slaps on the back.

BREATHING DIFFICULTIES

HYPERVENTILATION

What to look out for:
- rapid, deep and noisy breathing
- dizziness and confusion
- tingling in the hands

What to do:

1 Reassure casualty and, if possible, take them somewhere quiet and private to help them regain control of their breathing.

2 If hyperventilation continues, get the casualty to breathe into a paper bag.

IMPORTANT: Do not get the casualty to breathe into anything other than a paper bag.

INHALATION OF FUMES

What to look out for:
- difficulty in breathing
- coughing and wheezing
- in some cases: headache
  nausea
  blue skin
  confusion
  unconsciousness

What to do:

1 Send for an ambulance and, if appropriate, fire services.

2 If it is safe for you to do so, get the casualty away from danger and into fresh air.

3 Monitor the casualty's pulse and breathing until help arrives. Be ready to start *artificial ventilation* or *cardiopulmonary resuscitation*, if necessary.

What to look out for:
- red and blistered skin
- pain
- dark red, charred skin (in severe cases)
- *shock*

What to do:

1 Cool the affected area immediately under cold running water for at least 10 minutes.

2 If possible, remove any jewellery or loosen any constricting clothing.

3 Cover the burn with a sterile, non-fluffy dressing.

NEVER: burst blisters or apply creams, lotions or ointments to a burn.

IMPORTANT: chemical burns need prolonged washing.

Remember the priorities:

ABC

Airways

Breathing
and
Circulation

CHEST WOUNDS ⊙

What to look out for:
- pain and difficulty in breathing
- confusion
- shock
- coughing up blood
- blue lips and skin
- blood frothing out of a wound
- unconsciousness

What to do:

1 Cover the wound immediately with your hand or, if the patient is conscious, their hand.

2 Cover the wound with a sterile dressing. If the wound is deep, cover this dressing with a plastic bag or similar and make an airtight seal by sticking down the four sides down with tape or securing it with a bandage.

3 If the casualty is conscious get them to sit down, leaning slightly towards the side that is injured.

4 Send for an ambulance.

IMPORTANT:
If the casualty becomes unconscious, check they are still breathing and have a pulse, and put in the *recovery position* on their injured side. If breathing stops, start artificial ventilation and, if you lose a pulse, *cardiopulmonary resuscitation.*

CONCUSSION

What to look out for:
- unconsciousness
- dizziness and nausea
- loss of memory
- headache
- double-vision

What to do:

1 If the casualty is unconscious, check their airway, breathing and pulse and put them in the *recovery position*. If they do not regain consciousness after a few minutes, send for an ambulance. Be ready to start artificial ventilation or *cardiopulmonary resuscitation*, if necessary.

2 If the casualty is conscious, lie them down in a comfortable position until their condition improves.

IMPORTANT: advise anyone who has had a blow to the head and lost consciousness to see their doctor.

IN YOUNG CHILDREN

What to look out for:
- twitching, shaking or rigid body
- unconsciousness
- hot, flushed skin
- clenched fists
- difficulty in breathing

What to do:

1 Remove any nearby objects that may harm the child.

2 Remove their clothing and sponge the child with tepid water to cool them down.

3 Put the child in the *recovery position* if possible.

4 Send for an ambulance.

NEVER: restrain a child during a fit.

CONVULSIONS

EPILEPSY

What to look out for:
- twitching of limbs and eyelids
- confusion
- unconsciousness
- shaking or rigid body
- unusual breathing pattern
- clenched jaw
- frothing at the mouth

What to do:

1 If possible, try to ease the casualty's fall.

2 Place a cushion or similar under the casualty's head, remove any objects that may cause harm and loosen any tight clothing.

3 Allow the casualty to recover in their own time. If they are unconscious, place in the *recovery position.*

NEVER: restrain the casualty or put anything in their mouth.

IMPORTANT: if the convulsions last longer than 10 minutes, or if this is the casualty's first attack, send for an ambulance.

Remember the priorities:

ABC

Airways

Breathing
and
Circulation

CRUSH INJURIES

What to look out for:
- casualty trapped under heavy object
- *fractures*
- *internal bleeding*
- *shock*

What to do:

1 Release the casualty from the object as soon as possible.

2 Deal with any *bleeding* , *fractures*, *internal bleeding* or *shock*.

3 Send for an ambulance.

> **NEVER:** release a casualty who has been crushed for more than 10 minutes.

HIGH BLOOD SUGAR

What to look out for:
- dry skin
- rapid pulse
- difficulty in breathing
- strong thirst
- need to urinate frequently
- unconsciousness
- nausea
- acetone-smelling breath
- pain in abdomen

What to do:

1 The priority is to get the casualty to hospital. Send for an ambulance immediately.

2 If the casualty becomes unconscious, put them in the *recovery position* and check their breathing and pulse regularly. Be ready to start *artificial ventilation* and *cardiopulmonary resuscitation*, if necessary.

DIABETES

LOW BLOOD SUGAR

What to look out for:
- **faintness and weakness**
- **confusion**
- **pale, cold and clammy skin**
- **strong, rapid pulse**
- **shallow breathing**
- **hunger**

What to do:

1 Get the casualty to sit or lie down and give them a sugary drink such as orange juice, sweet tea or a couple of spoonfuls of sugar dissolved in a glass of water.

2 When they have recovered, give the casualty something sweet or starchy to eat and let them rest. You should also advise them to see their doctor.

IMPORTANT: If the casualty is unconscious, do not give them anything by mouth. Send for an ambulance. Put them in the *recovery position* and monitor their breathing and pulse. Be ready to start *artificial ventilation* or *cardiopulmonary resuscitation,* if necessary.

Remember the priorities:

ABC

Airways

Breathing
and
Circulation

DISLOCATIONS

What to look out for:
- pain made worse by movement
- difficulty in moving affected joint
- swelling and bruising
- *shock*
- unusual appearance of joint

What to do:

1 Rest and support the joint in the position which is most comfortable for the casualty.

2 Apply an ice pack or cold compress to affected area.

3 Ensure casualty is taken to hospital.

NEVER: try to push bones back into position.

NEVER: apply ice directly to bare skin – wrap it in a cloth first.

What to look out for:
- *hypothermia*
- unconsciousness

What to do:

1 Try to rescue the casualty but don't put yourself in danger. If possible, stay on dry land and reach out to the casualty with a stick, or throw a rope.

2 Try to keep the casualty's head lower than their chest once they are out of the water.

3 If the casualty has stopped breathing send for an ambulance and start *artificial ventilation* as soon as possible.

4 Clear any water from the stomach and air passages by placing them on their front, holding their waist and lifting their lower back. If the casualty has no pulse, start *cardiopulmonary resuscitation.*

5 If the casualty is breathing and has a pulse, put them in the *recovery position* and insulate from the cold.

6 If they are conscious, remove wet clothing, insulate from the cold and treat them for *hypothermia.* Monitor their breathing and pulse until help arrives.

NEVER: put yourself at risk – if in doubt, call the emergency services.

IMPORTANT: anyone who has lost consciousness should be advised to seek medical attention.

DRUG OVERDOSE

What to look out for:
- unconsciousness
- confusion
- faintness and dizziness
- difficulty in breathing
- vomiting

What to do:

1 Clear the airway, check breathing and pulse. Be ready to start *artificial ventilation* or *cardiopulmonary resuscitation*, if necessary.

2 If the casualty is unconscious but is breathing and has a pulse, put them in the *recovery position.*

3 Send for an ambulance and monitor the casualty's breathing and pulse until help arrives.

NEVER: try to make the casualty vomit.

IMPORTANT: Keep a sample of any vomited material to take to hospital with the casualty.

EAR INJURIES

What to look out for:
- pain
- bleeding from ear
- bloody, watery fluid leaking from ear
- loss of hearing (in some cases)

What to do:

1 Sit the casualty down, leaning their head over onto the injured side.

2 Cover the ear with a sterile dressing and get the casualty to hold it in place.

3 The casualty should be taken to hospital, keeping their head inclined to the injured side.

NEVER: plug the injured ear or insert anything into the ear canal.

IMPORTANT: bloody, watery fluid leaking from ear may indicate serious head injury. Urgent medical attention is required.

What to look out for:
- **unconsciousness**
- **burns**

What to do:

1 Only approach the casualty once the current is off or the contact is broken. If possible, switch current off at the mains. Break the contact between the electrical source and the casualty with something dry and non-conductive, such as a broom handle or a rolled up newspaper.

2 Check the casualty's breathing and pulse, and be ready to start *artificial ventilation* or *cardiopulmonary resuscitation* if necessary.

3 Call an ambulance.

IMPORTANT: if high voltage electricity is involved, call an ambulance and stay well clear of the area until help arrives.

CORROSIVE CHEMICALS

What to look out for:
- **pain**
- **swelling of eyelid**
- **red, swollen and/or watering eye**

What to do:

1 Gently hold the casualty's eye open under cold running water for at least 10 minutes. You could also use a jug or glass.

2 Cover the injured eye with a sterile dressing and secure with a bandage.

3 Ensure the casualty is taken to hospital.

NEVER: allow the casualty to touch their eye.

FOREIGN BODY IN THE EYE

What to look out for:
• pain
• twitching eyelid
• bloodshot and watering eye
• difficulty in seeing

What to do:

1 Gently separate the casualty's eyelids with your finger and thumb and look carefully for the foreign body.

2 Wash it out using an eye-bath or clean water from a glass.

3 If this is unsuccessful, try removing it with the damp corner of a clean handkerchief or cotton bud.

NEVER: attempt to remove anything embedded in the eye. Cover the eye with a sterile dressing and ensure the casualty is taken to hospital.

EYE WOUNDS

What to look out for:
- pain
- bleeding
- difficulty in seeing

What to do:

1 Get the casualty to lie on their back and keep their eyes as still as possible.

2 Cover the injured eye with a sterile dressing then secure with a bandage, covering both eyes to stop them moving the injured eye.

3 Ensure the casualty is taken to hospital.

NEVER: try to remove an embedded foreign body.

What to look out for:
- temporary loss of consciousness
- pale skin
- slow pulse

What to do:

1 Ensure the casualty is lying on their back. Raise their legs and loosen any tight clothing.

2 Make sure the casualty has some fresh air by opening a window, for example.

NEVER: place someone's head between their knees if they feel faint. If they do faint, their head is likely to hit the ground as they fall.

IMPORTANT: if unconsciousness lasts longer than a few minutes, call an ambulance and monitor casualty's breathing and pulse until help arrives.

FEVER

What to look out for:
- temperature above 37 °C (98.6 °F)
- pale, cold skin
- hot, clammy, flushed skin
- aches and pains
- headache

What to do:

1 Get the casualty to bed, making sure they rest and keep warm.

2 Give the casualty plenty of fluids to drink.

IMPORTANT: if the casualty's high temperature continues or if it rises above 40 °C (104 °F), seek the advice of a doctor urgently.

FRACTURES

What to look out for:
- intense pain, especially on movement of the injured area
- injured area looks odd and unnatural
- swelling and bruising
- difficulty in moving injured area
- *shock*

What to do:

1 Tell the casualty to keep still. If possible, do not move the injured area but steady and support it.

2 Any joints above and/or below the fracture must be immobilized to prevent further injury. Use a sling for arm fractures, which can be made from a triangular bandage, scarf, towel or similar.

3 Use splints to immobilize leg, upper arm, elbow, finger and wrist fractures. Any long, firm object may be used (for example an umbrella or rolled newspaper) with plenty of padding. In the case of leg fractures, you could also tie the casualty's legs together.

NEVER: try to straighten a broken limb.

IMPORTANT: if the fracture is open, control the *bleeding* and cover with a sterile dressing.

HEAD INJURIES ⓘ

What to look out for:
- headache
- nausea and vomiting
- unconsciousness
- memory loss
- bleeding
- convulsions
- difficulty in seeing

What to do:

1 If possible, try not to move the casualty as the injury may have affected their spine.

2 If the casualty is unconscious, open the airway, check breathing and pulse, and be ready to start *artificial ventilation* or *cardiopulmonary resuscitation*, if necessary. Send for an ambulance. Treat any other injuries, such as *bleeding*.

3 If conscious, treat possible *concussion*.

IMPORTANT: blows to the head should be treated seriously. Anyone who has been unconscious should seek medical attention.

Remember the priorities:

ABC

Airways

Breathing
and
Circulation

ANGINA PECTORIS

What to look out for:

- gripping pain in chest, often spreading to arm and jaw
- pain and/or tingling in the hand
- difficulty in breathing
- sudden weakness

What to do:

1 Sit the casualty down and give them any medication they may have to ease their condition.

2 The casualty should feel better within a few moments. If the pain continues or returns, call an ambulance. Monitor breathing and pulse closely and be ready to start *cardiopulmonary resuscitation* if necessary.

HEART DISORDERS ⚠

HEART ATTACK

What to look out for:
- persistent crushing pain radiating out from the chest
- difficulty in breathing
- faintness and dizziness
- cold clammy skin
- pale skin and blue lips
- rapid pulse which weakens
- sudden collapse
- confusion
- *shock*

What to do:

1 Sit the casualty down, supporting their head and bent knees with cushions or similar.

2 Call an ambulance. Check breathing and pulse regularly and be ready to start *cardiopulmonary resuscitation* if necessary.

CARDIAC ARREST

> **IMPORTANT:** if you have an ordinary aspirin and the casualty is conscious, give them one tablet to chew slowly.

What to look out for:
- no pulse
- no breathing

What to do:

1 Check the casualty's breathing and pulse.

2 If neither are present, send for an ambulance and start *cardiopulmonary resuscitation* immediately.

HEAT DISORDERS

HEAT EXHAUSTION

What to look out for:
- headache
- faintness and dizziness
- nausea
- clammy, pale skin
- rapid pulse which weakens
- difficulty in breathing
- cramps
- sweating

What to do:

1 Get the casualty to lie down, raise and support their legs. Loosen or remove any tight or heavy clothing.

2 Give the casualty a glass of water with a pinch of salt added to it, which they should sip slowly.

3 If the casualty becomes unconscious, put them in the *recovery position* and send for an ambulance. Check their breathing and pulse regularly until help arrives and be ready to start *artificial ventilation* or *cardiopulmonary resuscitation*, if necessary.

IMPORTANT: if the casualty's condition does not quickly improve or if they start to vomit, seek medical help immediately.

HEAT DISORDERS

HEATSTROKE

What to look out for:
- headache
- dizziness
- confusion
- hot, dry, flushed skin
- high temperature (above 40 °C/104 °F)
- nausea and vomiting
- rapid pulse
- unconsciousness

What to do:

1 Move the casualty to a cool place, loosen or remove any tight or heavy clothing.

2 Wrap the casualty in a sheet which has been dampened with cold water. Make sure the sheet stays wet and fan the casualty to keep them cool.

3 Check the casualty's temperature regularly. Once it has fallen to a safer level (under 40oC/100.4 oF) remove the wet sheet and stop the cooling process.

IMPORTANT: if the casualty becomes unconscious, put them in the *recovery position* and call an ambulance immediately. Check their breathing and their pulse regularly and be ready to start *artificial ventilation* or *cardiopulmonary resuscitation*, if necessary.

Remember the priorities:

ABC

Airways

Breathing
and
Circulation

HYPOTHERMIA

What to look out for:
- shivering
- cold, dry and pale skin
- confusion and lethargy
- slow pulse and breathing
- lack of coordination

What to do:

1 Move the person to a dry, warm place and remove any wet clothing, replacing it with warm, dry articles. If possible, wrap them in a blanket and cover their head.

2 If the casualty is conscious, give them a hot drink.

3 If the casualty becomes unconscious, put them in the *recovery position* and check their breathing and pulse regularly. Be ready to start *artificial ventilation* or *cardiopulmonary resuscitation*, if necessary.

NEVER: warm the casualty too quickly or extremely by putting them near a fire or using a hot water bottle, as this may cause *shock*.

NEVER: give the casualty alcohol.

Remember the priorities:

ABC

Airways

Breathing
and
Circulation

NOSE BLEEDS

What to look out for:
• bleeding from nose

What to do:

1 Sit the casualty down, with their head well forward, and ask them to breathe through their mouths and to avoid speaking, swallowing, coughing or sniffing.

2 Get them to pinch their nose just below the bridge.

3 After about 10 minutes, get them to release their nose. If the bleeding hasn't stopped, repeat the process for a further 10 minutes. If there is still no improvement, the casualty should be taken to hospital, still leaning forward and pinching their nose.

4 Once the bleeding has stopped, tell the casualty to avoid blowing their nose for a while.

IMPORTANT: if a bloody but pale fluid leaks from the nose or if the casualty is unconscious, medical attention should be sought immediately. If the casualty is unconscious, send for an ambulance, put them in the *recovery position* and monitor their breathing and pulse. Be ready to start *artificial ventilation* or *cardiopulmonary resuscitation,* if necessary.

POISONING

What to look out for:
- pain in digestive tract
- nausea and vomiting
- drowsiness and faintness
- confusion
- difficulty in breathing
- headache
- unconsciousness
- flushed, damp skin
- fever
- *shock*

What to do:

1 The main priority is to get the casualty to hospital.

2 If the casualty is unconscious, check the airway, breathing and pulse and put them in the *recovery position*. Call an ambulance and be ready to start *artificial ventilation* or *cardiopulmonary resuscitation*, if necessary.

3 Any vomited material or evidence such as syringes, suicide notes or pill bottles should be sent with the casualty to hospital.

4 If the poison has been absorbed through the skin, remove any contaminated clothing from the casualty (protecting yourself with rubber gloves) and wash the affected area thoroughly under running water.

NEVER: try to get the casualty to vomit, as it may cause further harm.

NEVER: give the casualty anything to eat or drink.

IMPORTANT: if you need to resuscitate the casualty, make sure that any poisonous substances have been washed away from their mouths.

IMPORTANT: if you are taking the casualty to the hospital by car, make sure someone calls the hospital casualty department to warn them of your arrival.

SEVERED LIMBS

What to do:

1 Control *bleeding* by raising limb and applying direct pressure.

2 Apply sterile dressing and secure with a bandage.

3 Treat the casualty for *shock* .

4 Send for an ambulance and warn them of nature of injury.

NEVER: apply a tourniquet to control bleeding.

What to do with severed limb:

1 Wrap the severed limb in kitchen film or put in a polythene bag.

2 Wrap this again in some soft material such as soft fabric and then place in another plastic bag, filled with crushed ice.

3 Note the time of the injury and the casualty's name and label the bag, which you should hand over to the medics when they arrive.

NEVER: Wash the severed limb or clean it with any antiseptic or disinfectant, wrap it in any material other than plastic or let it come in direct contact with ice.

Remember the priorities:

ABC

Airways

Breathing
and
Circulation

SHOCK (!)

What to look out for:
- rapid pulse which weakens
- pale, cold, clammy skin
- weakness and dizziness
- thirst
- nausea and vomiting
- confusion and anxiety
- unconsciousness
- rapid breathing

What to do:

1 If possible, treat any cause for the shock, such as severe *bleeding* or *burns*.

2 With the casualty lying on their back, raise and support their legs (unless you suspect *fractures*).

3 Loosen any tight clothing especially around the neck, chest and waist.

4 Ensure that the casualty is kept warm, but do not over-heat them – a blanket should be enough.

5 If the casualty becomes unconscious, put into the *recovery position*, monitor their breathing and pulse and be ready to start *artificial ventilation* or cardiopulmonary resuscitation, if necessary.

NEVER: give the casualty anything to eat or drink. If they are thirsty, just moisten their lips.

SPINAL INJURIES ⓘ

What to look out for:
- pain in the neck or at the level of the injury
- unusual-looking spine
- loss of sensation
- unusual sensations such as burning, tingling or heavy feeling in limbs
- difficulty in breathing
- loss of control over limbs or bodily functions

What to do:

1 Tell the casualty not to move. Do not move the casualty from the position in which they were found, unless they are unconscious or in danger where they are. Your aim is to prevent further damage to the spine or spinal cord.

2 Steady the casualty's head by placing your hands gently over their ears and keeping them there. If possible, get a bystander to pad the casualty's head and shoulders to protect them.

3 Send for an ambulance.

4 If the casualty becomes unconscious, put in the *recovery position*. If at all possible, do this with the help of at least 1 other person. It is essential to keep the casualty's head and torso aligned at all times. One person should control the position of the head and neck while the others move the lower part of the body, acting together. Once they are in the recovery position, ensure that the casualty is supported there until help arrives. Monitor the casualty's breathing and pulse and be ready to start *artificial ventilation* and *cardiopulmonary resuscitation*, if necessary.

NEVER: move a casualty, if at all possible, or pull on their neck.

IMPORTANT: if you are alone, remember that the first priority is to keep the casualty's airway open.

IMPORTANT: if you have no choice but to move the casualty, get as much help as you can – preferably four other people. One person should keep the casualty's head and neck in line with the rest of their torso, while the others roll the body on to a stretcher.

What to look out for:
- **pain**
- **restricted movement of joints**
- **swelling**
- **bruising**

What to do:
Remember: **RICE**

      Rest injured area
      Ice or cold compress
      Compression bandage
      Elevate injured area

1 Remove any restrictive clothing or footwear from the injured area.

2 Get the casualty to take any weight pressure off the injured area: they should rest and support it.

3 Apply ice or a cold compress to reduce the pain, swelling and bruising.

4 Apply gentle, even pressure by bandaging the injured area; then raise and support it.

5 Ensure the casualty goes to hospital or sees their doctor.

Remember the priorities:

ABC

Airways

Breathing
and
Circulation

What to look out for:
- difficulty in breathing
- unconsciousness
- blue skin
- prominent veins in face
- constriction marks around neck

What to do:

1 Remove anything which is stopping the casualty from breathing, being careful to support their neck (in the case of a constricted airway); or move them into the fresh air.

2 Call an ambulance.

3 If the casualty becomes unconscious, place in *recovery position* check their breathing and pulse and be ready to start *artificial ventilation* or *cardiopulmonary resuscitation*, if necessary.

IMPORTANT: do not tamper with any evidence (such as ropes or suicide notes).

STROKE ⓘ

What to look out for:
- sudden headache
- confusion
- unconsciousness
- paralysis or weakness, usually on one side of the body
- severe headache
- strong pulse
- difficulty in speaking
- seizures (in some cases)
- loss of control of bodily functions

What to do:

1 Get the casualty to lie down with their head and shoulders raised slightly, supported against some pillows or similar.

2 Loosen any tight clothing, keep the person warm and use a clean cloth to absorb any dribbling.

3 If the casualty becomes unconscious, place in the *recovery position*, monitor their breathing and pulse, and be ready to start *artificial respiration* and *cardiopulmonary resuscitation*, if necessary.

4 Send for an ambulance.

NEVER: give the casualty anything to eat or drink.

Remember the priorities:

ABC

Airways

Breathing
and
Circulation

Part 2
FIRST AID
EMERGENCY PRIORITIES

FIRST AID EMERGENCY

Understanding and observing the first aid priorities saves lives.

DO

- Get help as soon as possible.
- Learn the life-saving techniques (described in this section) from a trained instructor – St John's Ambulance and the Red Cross run courses.
- Remember that every moment is vital: act quickly and calmly
- Reassure casualty by talking to them
- Keep a first aid kit

DON'T

- Wait for an emergency to occur – read this book now!
- Approach a casualty until you have checked it is safe to do so.
- Delay getting a seriously injured casualty to hospital – dealing with their trivial injuries wastes valuable time.
- Move a casualty unless it is necessary for safety.
- Leave a casualty alone if you can send someone else for help.
- Give a casualty anything to eat or drink.

ACTION AT AN EMERGENCY

Remember the priorities:
DANGER
RESPONSE
AIRWAY
BREATHING
CIRCULATION

In the event of an emergency, ask yourself the following questions:

Is there any Danger?
- Only approach a casualty once you are sure that there is no danger for you, the injured person or bystanders.
- Assess the resources available to you: are there any qualified medical professionals or any bystanders who could help you?
- If you can, make the area safe, remembering to put your own safety first. Do not attempt to deal with a life-threatening hazard.

Is there any Response from the casualty?

If the casualty is conscious:
- assist into a comfortable position
- check for injury and illness
- treat as appropriate
- seek medical help, if necessary

If the casualty is unconscious, ask yourself the following questions:
- Is there something blocking the casualty's Airway?
- Check the casualty's mouth for any obstructions and ensure the airway is open (see Open the Airway)

Is the casualty Breathing?

YES

1 treat any life-threatening injury
2 put casualty into the *recovery position*
3 get help
4 check their breathing and pulse frequently.

NO

1 If you are not alone, send someone for an ambulance.

ACTION AT AN EMERGENCY

Is there a pulse (i.e. is the casualty's blood Circulating)?

YES

1 If you are alone, start *artificial ventilation* immediately.

2 Once you have given 10 breaths, call an ambulance.

3 Continue artificial ventilation at the rate of 10 breaths a minute until help arrives. Check breathing and pulse after every 10 breaths.

NO

1 Call an ambulance immediately.

2 Begin *cardiopulmonary resuscitation* at the rate of 2 artificial ventilation breaths to 15 chest compressions, until help arrives.

FOR LIFE-THREATENING SITUATIONS

Assessing the casualty

Remember: Airway
Breathing
Circulation

Check Response

1 Ask a question or command, for example: 'Can you hear me?', 'What is your name?' or 'Open your eyes'.

2 If you get no response, gently shake the casualty's shoulders.

3 If there is still no response, the casualty is unconscious. If someone is with you, send them for an ambulance.

Open the Airway

1 Ensuring that the airway is clear is of paramount importance. Deprivation of air, even for a few minutes, can be fatal or cause brain damage. Everything else is of secondary importance.

FOR LIFE-THREATENING SITUATIONS

2 Remove any obvious obstructions from the mouth, such as vomited material or loose dentures.

3 With two fingers under the casualty's chin and your other hand steadying their forehead, gently tilt their head back.

Check for Breathing
With your face close to the casualty's mouth:

1 Look for the chest rising and falling

2 Listen for the sounds of breathing

3 Feel for their breath on your cheek

FOR LIFE-THREATENING SITUATIONS

Check for a pulse (Circulation)

1 Place two finger tips in the hollow between the casualty's Adam's apple and the large neck muscle. Feel for five seconds before you decide that there is no pulse.

2 If there is breathing and a pulse, put casualty in the *recovery position*.

3 If there is a pulse but no breathing, start *artificial ventilation*.

4 If there is no pulse present, start *cardiopulmonary resuscitation*.

THE RECOVERY POSITION

Any unconscious casualty that is breathing and has a pulse should be placed in the *recovery position* as it prevents the tongue from falling back and blocking the throat, and reduces the risk of the casualty choking on their own vomit. The following description assumes that the casualty is on their back. You may therefore find that not all the steps are necessary, depending on the position the casualty is in.

1 Kneel facing the casualty's chest and remove any spectacles or bulky objects from their pockets.

2 Ensure their airway is open by lifting their chin (see Open the Airway).

3 Position the arm which is nearest to you at right angles to the casualty's body, with the elbow bent and palm facing out.

4 Bring the casualty's other arm across their chest, placing the back of their hand against the cheek which is nearest to you and holding it there.

5 With your other hand, grasp the leg which is furthest from you at the thigh, pulling the casualty's knee up with their foot flat on the ground.

6 Still with your hand keeping the back of their hand against their cheek, gently press down on the lower thigh with your other hand, thus rolling the casualty towards you, on their side.

7 Again, ensure the airway is open by tilting the casualty's head back.

8 If necessary, adjust the uppermost leg so that the hip and knee are bent at right angles for stability.

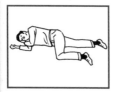

9 Call an ambulance.

IMPORTANT: if you suspect *spinal* or *head injuries*, it is dangerous to move a casualty except under the supervision of a skilled and knowledgeable person.

1 Ensure the casualty's airway is clear (see Open the Airway) and turn them on their back.

2 Pinch the casualty's nostrils between your index finger and thumb to close the airway.

3 Take a deep breath and with your mouth open, place it over the casualty's mouth, ensuring that you have made a good seal.

4 Blow steadily into the casualty's mouth (for about 2 seconds). You should see the casualty's chest rising.

5 Remove your mouth and allow the chest to fall.

6 Repeat this process until help arrives or the casualty starts breathing again.

If the chest does not rise check that:
- There is no obstruction to the airway (see below)
- The head is tilted far back
- There is a firm seal around the casualty's mouth
- The nostrils are firmly closed

Clearing an obstruction:

1 Check the mouth for any obstruction.

2 Slap casualty's back firmly to dislodge obstruction.

3 Give abdominal thrusts by kneeling astride the casualty, and, with one hand on top of the other, pushing sharply just under their ribcage.

IMPORTANT: the risk of transmission of disease during artificial ventilation is low for the person giving first aid.

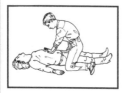

BABIES AND CHILDREN UNDER 8
It is advisable when giving artificial ventilation to babies and small children to place your mouth over both their nose and mouth.

IMPORTANT: breathe gently, providing just enough air to make the child's chest rise.

If the casualty has stopped breathing and has no pulse, it is essential to start CPR immediately. It is preferable for this to be done by two people, as it is a very tiring procedure.

1 Send for an ambulance, if you are not alone.

2 Ensure the casualty's airway is clear (see Open the Airway) and that they are lying flat on their back.

3 Give 5 *artificial ventilations*. If you are alone, call an ambulance now.

4 With one hand, find the casualty's lowest rib, sliding your finger to the point where the ribs meet the breastbone. Place your middle finger over this point and your index finger just above it.

5 Place the heel of your other hand above your two fingers. This is the area where you will be applying pressure.

6 Place the heel of your first hand on top of the hand which is now correctly positioned and interlock the fingers.

7 Keeping your arms straight, lean over the casualty and press down vertically and firmly on the breastbone so that it is depressed about five centimetres (two inches). Do this firmly and evenly, fifteen times in ten seconds and then give two full *mouth-to-mouth ventilations*

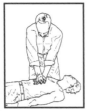

8 Continue until help arrives or the pulse returns.

IMPORTANT: if there is someone with you who can help, the ratio is 1 breath to every 5 compressions.

CHEST COMPRESSIONS FOR A BABY

What to do

1 Find the correct position for your index and middle fingers by imagining a line drawn between the baby's nipples and placing your fingers just below the mid-point of this line.

2 Using your fingers, press about 2 cm down (just under 1 inch) at the rate of about 15 every 10 seconds. Remember that chest compressions should be combined with *artificial ventilation* using the ratio of 5 compressions to 1 breath.

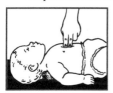

What to do:

1 Find the correct position for your hand in the same way as you would an adult (see above).

2 Using one hand only, press about 3 cm down (just over 1 inch) at the rate of about 15 compressions every 10 seconds. Remember that chest compressions should be combined with *artificial ventilation*, using the ratio of 5 compressions to 1 breath.

FAMILY HEALTH DETAILS/NOTES

Name . . . .

Blood Group . . . .

Medical conditions . . . .

Allergies . . . .

Special medication . . . .

Name . . . .

Blood Group . . . .

Medical conditions . . . .

Allergies . . . .

Special medication . . . .

FIRST AID BOX

First aid kits can be kept in the home, car and workplace. Make sure you:

- keep it in a waterproof box
- label it clearly
- store it in a dry place (bathrooms for instance are often too damp)
- replace any items as you use them
- keep this book with your kit for quick reference